The Angel of History

The Angel of History

poems by

Mark Wilson

LEAKY BOOT PRESS

The Angel of History
by Mark Wilson

First published in 2013 by
Leaky Boot Press
http://www.leakyboot.com

ISBN: 978-1-909849-08-2

Contents

ONE

In Principio
after Arvo Pärt

1

A book of beginnings;
      proof-read
     manuscript of connoted
departures.

An illuminated codex implies
    a periplum or
sea-voyage.

Castor, Pollux; these sins
    of the fathers piling up
like metaphysical
road-kill.

Ostentatiously
    bringing out firstfruits,
knowing full well
    the best is still
        garnered within.

To be seated six-square
    within the temple: the
perfected youthful family
      as model and
         set-square.

As their invisible halos
    still project

from pre-ordained
           precision.

Take in this exquisite relief:

Philemon and Baucis:
      spiritual caretakers of
      their ubiquitous
           house-meeting.

Like two linden-trees
      columned either side of
      their supernal
           threshold.

One nursing the other in
      the nested dark of the
      adytum.

Suppliants all,
      striving for prophetic
charisma within the geometric
      chiasmus of a
           golden cosmos.

Musty red hymnals
      were pocket-sized apertures
      to a puritanical
           paradiso.

Stained-glass windows
      being the grandiose
           no-no.

Lexicons of
      self-molested child-poets;
seven years old
      and already Pythagorean
        and counting.

Vehicles of our transfiguration

tripped up with a
　　　guilty implication.

As axle-rods of original sin
　　shear through the
　　　　symbolic baldachins.

Having their *san graal*
　　filled at the
　　　　ecclesiastical nipple.

Having their ultimate fill;
　　what heady bloodless
　　　　sacrifice
　　　　　was there?

In antiquity the priest was
　　as much the town butcher
　　as he was the
　　　　town priest.

As, chiliastically,
　　I envision the seamless,

this inexplicable synthesis
　　of Gethsemene and

　　　　The Enneads.

2

Demiurgus in three
　　distinct movements;

intricate
　　fretwork-traceries over
　　this deafening
　　　　void.

Emanation of pure *nous* is
　　heliographically

11

curved, so
    multi-faceted.

'Demiurgus' suggesting
    the binary creative
        urge;

a movement akin to
    an oscillating ellipse
        so it appears.

What spinning coherence
    stammers erratic from
        our logos of
            re-beginnings?

Certainly not *le mot juste*
    or the word for the
word's sake;
        surely.

Through the 12 houses of
    terrae have we
        reluctantly come.

For your *nekuia* is
    absolutely necessary
in this absurd
        continuum.

As those asphodel–strewn
    playing fields along the

embankment were the
    Arcadian pastures
        of a mislaid
           innocence.

For the monad had indeed
    become the demiurge
with its sheer projection

of a binary
                    nous.

That mystery was transacted
        within a silver bowl,
within a silver goblet
                    no less.

Those emblems proffered
        by an enervated
Earthshaker to your
        trembling, Odyssean lips.

As you played a minor
        prophet with your
        erratically cadenced
                    tongue.

Knowing that mimetic
        mysterium deep within your

psyche would one day
        overcome the multitudinous
millstones piling up to
                    entomb posterity in.

This incipient miracle
        always to be quelled in
                    that ultimate

                    quarantine.

3

Principally, the first
        breath is the most
        conclusive;

our prelude is, in this
        instance, an uncanny

similitude of our
                    postlude.

There is an intelligence
        to all this that
arrestingly comes
                shining through.

Like the distillation of
                    pure ambience.

A premier pulchritude,
            Dante's most alert

Lord of Love; sheer
        magnetism of the first
                beloved's pupils

accounts, I'm sure,
            for certain
                    phenomena.

Inscribed configurations,
        looser laser-etchings;

delineated Sophia and other
        goddesses of our vast
                empyrean.

I surrender neither the
        temples nor the iconostases,

despite their man-made
        tendency to trammel in
                        deity.

Apollonius not admitted
        to the mysteries' initiation
and other such
                fallacious ironies.

God's fools,
        the dogged gait of
bedraggled versifiers

        welcome to no inner
sanctum; and yet
        cosmic communicants
                        everywhere.

And that Paul's epistles
        lacked a coherent
cosmology always a
                juncture to
                        differ.

Instead, my soul
        too much kindled by

the logos of the
                Koine Johannine.

Dredged up throughout
        infanthood never to
                        desert;

like a purgatorial fire
        sent with an express
purpose and exemplifying
                        radiance.
My upper body is in
        paradise; my lower body

resides in the
                scurrilous

                        quotidian.

The Lord's Supper

after Jerome Rothenberg's *Poland/1931:The Wedding*

this psyche is stuffed with hymnals
little red hymnals musty red psalters
they have even brought out the silver chalice
with the silver spout
the three silver goblets
the three silver serving-bowls
they have sipped ruby juices of the vine
this bread is white-powdery instantly honey-sweet
they are seated in a formal row of six
the young most youthful family
in one archaic block measured out in milli-cubits
by one loved one respected elder
the women's heads are all covered
head-scarves berets gossamer veils sunday-best
they have brought out the small wooden
collection-boxes the silk-tailored moneybags
standing sentinel on the central table or dais
no more an altar but a festal board
the lord's supper the holy communion of the lamb

this psyche is stuffed replete with ambivalence
as I intake a smidgeon of bread a sip of claret
holiness pervades in an almost
psycho-somatic fashion
but this psyche is stuffed
with more than red hymnals

for I have had my fill

The Elders

after Geoffrey Hill's *The Apostles: Versailles, 1919*

The Elders sat in the upper
room. They cogitated.
Spiritual repast for the
beleaguered flock was

not scarce in their well-
swept garner. Dispensation
will follow dispensation,
but the gilded rapture has

air-lifted their pneumatic
bodies to yet another
supernal terrene. I see
them now as in an

incandescent column: the
rotund, the lean, the
stocky hungering for pre-
eminence in that hierarchy.

Salt and grain spilt in their
wake; their sub-solar
charges cowered in the
atrium. Principalities

winced behind the scarlet
proscenium. The Elect
were ticked present on
ingress. The fewer the

better.

King of the Jews

The stylus of flame
is in your hand. You
are scribal in your
diligence, O master of

the parchment-scrolls.
You have contrived
ideograms of ink with
a celerity that marks you

out, with a distinction
of semantic choice
which is most to be
admired. There are

icons to be lifted up,
icons to be broken on
lintels and thresholds.
You have traced out a

messianic poetics that
will displace kingdoms
and principalities. For
you are that charismatic

voice in a ganglion
of chaos and your
glossolalia will rise
above their incoherent

shibboleths to create
new temple-liturgy.
At the end of yet
another innovative

day you will walk by
the Dung Gate and not
notice that old man
shovelling up excrement

of his only cow.

TWO

The Angel of History
for Patrick Anderson, James Taylor and Ian Wells

'A Klee drawing named *Angelus Novus* shows an angel looking as though he is about to move away from something he is fixedly contemplating. His eyes are staring, his mouth is open, his wings are spread. This is how one pictures the angel of history. His face is turned toward the past. Where we perceive a chain of events, he sees one single catastrophe that keeps piling ruin upon ruin and hurls it in front of his feet. The angel would like to stay, awaken the dead, and make whole what has been smashed. But a storm is blowing from Paradise; it has got caught in his wings with such violence that the angel can no longer close them. The storm irresistibly propels him into the future to which his back is turned, while the pile of debris before him grows skyward. This storm is what we call progress.'

Walter Benjamin,
"Ninth Thesis on the Philosophy of History"

'History is a nightmare from which I am trying to awake.'

Stephen Dedalus in
"Ulysses" by James Joyce

The Angel of History (I)

Olives and tambourines;

predictive texts of stilted Academe.

The Angel of History
    bartering our youthful
wine-skins for these
        sacks of burlap.

Merlot. Shiraz. Ursula.
The wizardry of the squeezed
      muscatel.

We lose ourselves briefly in
    the tropical simmer of
        their glacial kingdom.

End of the sacrament, that
      undulating love-feast.

Dada and Vorticism emerge,
    scarred, but marginally
      triumphant.

The Angel of History is always
    on the move. We have
heard incessant rumours:

free-form, elliptical, syncopated
    even.

As Beatrice drifts imperiously
    away; whilst he clings, an
emaciated Odysseus, to the
    railings of the
        Old Kent Road.

With all the bohemians of the
    Golden Calf in tow.

The Angel of History has not
    yet passed us over.

Wait a second. Now he has.

Cry Dada

Cry Dada. Burn on the acute
    cylinders of the vortex.

Timon and John Amos Darby
    in a dynamic mesh of
        this triple self-portrait.

Their souls were made of
    medium-density-fibreboard;

that syllabus was a blinkered
    mule sick on Bloomsbury.

Compact, solidus: the dramatic
    heave of her *décolleté*

more sensuous than the Beatrice
    girl. More like Aquitaine and
those of her feminine ilk
        and curvature.

Love-courts of Ventadorn
    were spawned prodigious.

Take this dulcimer just this
    once and *try* to play in
        rhythm.

Mystically grazing on the *Maestà*
    whilst your hysterically
empty stomach waxes with both
        gnosis & pleasure.

You are not a cypher. Neither are
      you a primed pawn edging
out of this beleaguered kingdom.

Into the terrain of *l'avventura*
      have you come.

Cry Dada; the renewed glossolalia
      on your barbed tongue.

Ride a thousand vortexes in and
      out of our blackened sun.

Cry Dada; and make sense out
      of this spinning orb which
some erroneously believe is a

          terra firma.

Stigmatised Troubadors

River-citadel: this gargantuan
      pinball-machine gridlocking
its projectiles all around you.

He left a dessicated rose in
      the petite shoe she left behind
in his hall-of-residence room; shortly
      after that stomach-heaving
          boat party.

Waking up in an acute delirium
      within Wittenberg's cold cell
and instantly pulling on an
      inky cloak to fathom
          that atmosphere.

The stigmatised troubadours in
      all their accoutrements
          of drag.

Pound and Mina Loy make out
in the chiaroscuro of the
British Museum cloakroom
whilst H.D. sits oblivious
in the tearoom.

Bring out those home-grown,
familial truths wholesale
to the festal board. It's high time
for an ancestral reckoning.

With all the hermaphrodite
bohemians of the Golden Calf
you have reached your node of
Dionysian self-discovery.

Non-plussed, with an Apollonian
swagger, this former assumption
is discredited almost
immediately.

The Golden Calf

The undulating bodies of
unadulterated glam;
youthful, diversely
beautiful.

Lucian Freud's model dances
ample, with his wooden
block in tow.

Lords of strut and sham;
ladies of black mascara strapped
into their burlesque-
exquisite gowns.

The ghosts of Epstein and Gill
flicker with abrupt

sensuality in all their
vibrant loins.

The apprentice poet still agog
with the chutzpah-excitement
of unfermented youth.

One girl a mistress, the
other a muse.

Janey Morris, Lizzie Siddal
will arrive here shortly after
midnight; but Persephone
is still lost within
her lacquered underworld.

Antediluvian; a simmering hell
beneath the very enamelled
tiles of Elysium.

The stigmatised troubadours
climb on to their amplifiers
and wear Mephistopheles-
horns.

She is the paradigmatic apple
of his unfocusing eye; her
contours are quite unrepeatable
both in art and nature.

Orpheus' maenad smashed to
within ten feet of
oblivion.

The Angel of History (II)

The Angel of History is
wilfully perverse. His
distorted convex mirror
is actually concave.

Hindsight is like looking
      at the atom of a gnat through
the wrong end of an antique
      Hubble telescope.

Its opaque, circular lens is warped
      beyond the most astute
         human calculation.

It tells us next to nothing;
      is wilfully obscurantist.

And yet we are within a
      whisker of touching
      home-grown,
         celestial truth.

His mottled wing like the
      outer crust of some antedated
tabernacle levitates above
      our inert, prostrate bodies;

before smother-kissing us
      back to the
         grave.

Day of the Locusts

Restoration after the sheer
locust-plunge; this age
      of self-invention
         and wonder.

Ecstatic dictionaries opened to
      reveal woodcuts of the
         impossible.

Emerging from deep-set
      repression, hazy innocence.

That burnished mystic in your
eyes (so hazel) could never
                   really diminish.

A kingdom of paralytics
                   and doubters?

John Amos Darby keen as a
          succinct knife-blade. Watch
out when the post-structuralists
          snap you open!

Charing Cross Road: only one
          Station of a Truer Cross.

Dragging the carcass of urban
          isolation all the way back
                   to a provincial abattoir.

Kafkan tunnels where you
          unconsciously trundled.

Failing better was always
leitmotif of all Dadaistic
                   gestures.

That dumb-show is over;
And all that is left is this
          ferocious
                   fin-de-partie.

Kafkan Tunnels

Amos K. frisked of his hyper-
          sensitivity by masked
                   border-guards.

Took a trip to the turreted
academy for therapeutic-
          spiritual reasons known
                   only to his higher-self.

Hourglass sanatoriums littered
the post-punk landscape.

Unkempt, semen-stained beds
were exhibited in pristine galleries
patronised by the *nouveau riche.*

Whilst angelic battalions patrolled
the nocturnal streets and
turned up at halloween burlesques
in various occult disguises.

Interminable Kafkan tunnels
where you unconsciously trundle.
Time being ultimately
inconsequential.

The streets gave up their dead
at the rapture of your
ultimate panic.

There were forbidden urban zones
where White Mariahs squealed;
mewling for those real pastoral
scenes of Arcadian
tranquillity.

So it all must come down to that
elemental book-of-hours
where you happen to perceive the
legible Aleph streaming through

like a celestial ladder.

For the rest
is merely a babel of

non-sequiturs.

The White Mariah

It annunciates the hinge of
        each dispensation;

squealing like the Angel of
History himself after yet another
        routine guillotining.

Your customised womb-coma
        liveried with cream and
feather-down is a soteriological
        act.

The shuttling pulse of that
        urban gridlock; a white
blood cell ensuring the Balm-

of-Gilead reaches you as
        recorded-and-signed
                delivery.

Knowing the times and
seasons of your multi-various
        malevolencies; minutely

timing its arrivals-and-departures
        accordingly.

A spirit-level for the bio-chemically
        imbalanced ones; always
seeming to provide the required
            inner-sanctums.

Under gantries and advertising
plasmas
        have we come.

Entering the City of David with
        a Song of Ascents on our
           burgeoning tongue.

So up the hill of hourglass
sanatoriums are we
                    escalating.

Pilgrims of the Psychological
            Traumas; lost tribe of a

messianic kingdom that could
            never really happen in the
imagination of this *res publica*.

Let be; even the chanson of this
White Mariah has no end-stop,
            no real termination.

It is an enjambment of the mind's
            outrageous incredulity;

In short: an eternal
                    procrastination.

The Return

Emaciated, to within a sculpted
                    millimetre.

These circumscribed contours,
            purged perimeters.

Fragile gnostic surmisings
                    multiply.

Raskolnikov-eyed: the eternal,
            enervated student
                    approaching.

Susurrus of survival instincts
waft up to Dada heavens
            merely to transmogrify into
a precipitation of
                    phylacteries.

So: transpose the psalter into
a modern idiom in the spirit
        of Pound's *Confucius*
        or Logue's *Homer*...

And other such tests of the fledgling
        inventor's imagination.

Before you return from limbo's
hot gates:
                know thy calling.

Days of the Ingathering

That cunning thread, sinew
of artifice; your mystical
        preoccupation amongst

the masterfully-arranged icons
        has alchemised the *mezzo*
                del cammin false move.

Unclassifiable as the most
abstract, programmatic music
        can dare to be.

A defiant reconfiguration, this
ingathering of the most precious
        grain from the stubborn,
recalcitrant
                        earth-basin.

An elemental reconstruction
in the bare-naked face of the
        perturbed
                Angel of History.

Both you and he are still quite
        drenched in this

latter latter rain.

For a refusal to end-stop is a
mark of dispensational
                                character.

Every prophet, caught in the
precipitation of divine frenzy, has
            been made intimate with this
                        pellucid truth-pearl.

Furthermore, it's still a bead
            of transcendental

                        *in*comprehension.

The Angel of History (III)

Hands outspread; wings are
merely stumps of celestial
            marrow with a few
creamy tufts
                        fluttering.

As Klee depicts in
                        watercolour.

So you run from the
            enveloping horror unable
to pick out history's
                        survivors.

No, you must turn, eyes
widening: a slave to the
                        kalendar's dictums.

Turn from the human ovens,
            the scarred lowlands where
a few locals are searching for
            their murdered
                        pretty ones.

35

So you are passing over like
      an Asrael of predetermination.

And not even Walter Benjamin
      can describe the modulations
of your wings' enforced
          levitations.

For we must follow soon after
      in the slipstream of
your dying fall, over the pained
      thresholds of all temporal-
         spatial conundrums;

as if we ourselves were that
      gradation of purging

          flame-tongues.

THREE

Earth
after Aleksander Dovzhenko's *Earth*

Orchard of ripe precipitation;
baptism of gleaming apples.

A languorous season
when your skin was

redolent of smooth soil, salt-tang
of sweat. When the chronic

machine hadn't yet interposed
itself between you and the

      animate-source.

The Library Hovers Above Solaris
after Andrei Tarkovsky's *Solaris*

1

Parables have taught me much
about parallel universes; but you,
        beloved, may merely be the
fabrication of that ocean-planet,
                Solaris, for all I know.

A sylph-like muse of my own
fabled memorialising; my sweet,
        archetypical suspect
                paraded on an icon.

So we gather in the library:
Scientists, Writers, Stalkers all...
        to toast mankind? Punctual
as Halley's Comet have we
        come; in a green blaze of
                stillborn publicity.

And who is to distinguish us
in the ultimate levitation that
        transcends all intercourses?

Brueghel's *Hunters in the Snow*
        our clarion call...

                but who discerned?

Organ-preludes as our microcosm
then. Praeludium-and-fugue

departing one solar-system...
escalating the space-time curve...
nebulous curtains veil the
objective vision.

There is no such 'place' as the
holy-of-holies it seems in
outer, or inner, space. Hallowed
sanctums have proven to be a
movable feast whichever way
you squint through the
Hubble.

Technologies can only accelerate
our universal blindness into a far
deeper blindness with far more
high-definition detail.

Let me warm my palms in the
magnetic waves; accompanied
only by you,
my chapped-lipped,
beautiful one.

2

Bronze stallion huffs in ultramarine
meadow. Return of the prodigals
time and time over. The sheer
revelation of colour; a pellucid
'otherness' it seems.

Can the camera sculpt in
astrophysical time?

Shall we readily find ourselves
in liquid light when we're the
very hemispheres
of darkness?

Globular,
      fluid in our elusiveness,
      our last-ditch
          defensiveness.
Lux Aeterna a vague gnostic
              secret then?

So we pace around the half-
developed garden, kind of a loose-
      knit family; contemplate the
imminent voyages of tomorrow.

Burn documentation, shred
photographs. Paraphernalia of
      our paralysis preserved;
purged eerily at each
          suspected juncture.

The boredom is unique to every
innate situation it appears. For
      I have taught myself the
internal precipitation that defies
          all chemical logic.

Caught in the vacuum where even
      you prove a distant satellite, dear.

Ensconced in your heavenly
      throne-chariot; waiting
      uncomfortably

          for that scroll-recital
              to end.

3

Archaic leather wherein we reside;
buffed candelabras with two,
      maybe three candles
          sputtering.

You choose one ancient, dusty
tome for me to recite from;
      Civilisation's secretions flake
away regardless. And the Word is
    snugly cocooned within
            its ancient chrysalis.

Your fleshed-out apparition appears
within my sterile cabin most evenings.
    Exquisite, those familiar
curvatures; those alert
    summoners of my arousals.

Traced as if in a Leonardo painting,
    or within a futuristic photograph.

Lenses and filters that have not
even been invented or, at least,
      perfected yet.

Your breath within the adjacency
of my ear. A hot flux of hieroglyphs
    is surely forthcoming.

With hindsight, I have decided to
call this planet:
        Tantalisation.

As you hang a rustic cardigan on
this astro-chair, nose snuffing
    like an unperturbed doe...

As I turn over on the polyurethane
bed; look away towards the
      sliding doors.

Solaris seethes,
    Atlantean,
        not far below.

4

So we have come to this floating
library with our inquisitions, our
     heresies, our good intentions
for building
       Civilisation.

Seducers of the tongue caught
in intricate constellations
     (whether chosen or not).

Marble busts of Plato, Aristotle,
the great Kung (cast in jade)
     staple-pinion our multi-media
       research-centre.

Statues of Buddha in ubiquitous lotus
position; gilded icons of the Great
     Pantocrator; Christus hanging
gnarled upon a tree; Krishna
amorously embracing the
     well-endowed
        Radha.

And all the avatars and archangels
that have ever walked with the
     children of men leave their
phantasmal imprint on some
       shelf or table.

Even you are Saraswati or
Magdalene in the right light or
     atmosphere: mistress of
        fluidity.

And maybe that's what you really
are rather than a mere simulacrum.
     Moving eloquent beyond the
script; this tyranny of
       proscription.

Solaristics at an impasse.
Humankind at an impasse.

Let be   let be   let be.
Levitate regardless
      with (or without)

           candelabra
             and Tolstoy.

5

Confined laboratories of the
clonal over-assumption; five-year
      plans of the *Übermenschen*.

The discreetly hid, misshapen
midget, the two-headed sheep in a
      formaldehyde tank and other
such sub-human
          abominations.

Something terrible may have
      crawled out of the sea, before
          quickly mutating.

Scylla and Charybdis provoked
      to epic whirlpool consternations.

Solaris belching out like a wounded
      behemoth with irreplaceable
          horn crumpled.

Antiochus has polluted the temple
it seems; for toxic snow now hovers
      with incandescent deadliness.

The illuminated book slowly burns
in at the corners. The sacrosanct
      ash floats, chokes even the

energetic and the young...

Yet we remain
    cabined, cribbed within this
microcosmic library.
    Gravitation no longer
        restrains us.

And you remain as tangible to me
    as even the dictates of
        the
            maternal
                uterine.

6

After Rublev's *Apokalypse*, the
    cyber-exterminations;
that liquidation to end all
        liquidations.

Will the odyssey surely conclude
with some sort of homecoming
    (prodigal or otherwise)?

Prepared as a bride...
    coming down from heaven...
indeed, what
        Shekinah annunciations?

After the feverish,
    hallucinative vision when
the universe swelled agonised
beyond its usual
        eternal measure.

What of *Caritas*,
        greater than all these?

And what if we should penetrate

the heliosphere?
                    What then?

Another dying star to appropriately
name after some Classical
                    or Jazz composer?

Some other frontier or promised
land to politically
                    capitalise upon?

For the laws of deeds and ownership
seem to exist just as much in
          deep space as *terra firma*.

Solaris oozes its milk and honey
                    in Newtonian glory.

(Possibly, you're more to me than all
          Science could ever mean)

Maybe. Most of the time.
                    Spatially speaking.

Eucharistic:
          your emblems,
                    your technology,
                              girl.

For I will never quite get used to
          all your timeless 'resurrections'.

As Solaris simmers Atlantean
          below, spewing up

          islands of
                    paradise

                    and hell.

The Zone
after Andrei Tarkovsky's *Stalker*

1

timbre-rattle
the diesel-express
three sleeping
incumbents

tryst-appointment
vocational
      clandestine

post-nuclear?
      a meteor?

dolly-tracks
submerged
venomous syringe
Van Eyck's *Baptist*

pouring Vladivostok
a vodka libation?

hanged himself
        in situ

waterfall fluid
cenotaph anti-
christ messianic
      undertones
strutting beneath

thorny crowns

elect calling?
squeezing haemorrhoids?

last gashed well
in scarified
                universe

send-deliver
sibling didymus
into meatgrinder

spare no-one
redeem the
redeemed from
zealous sanctimony

there and
        back again?

2

inculcate scabrous
            ceremonies
black dog Emmaus

Stalker's limp hand
partially in scum

soviet quarantine

a proletarian sepia
unthawed cold war
                arcana

flotsam jetsam all
nexus-confined
            revelatory

Scientist-Stalker-Writer
the triad holy unholy
don't forget the
                    jerry-can

leant-on formica
has the Zone
spawned abnormality?

a deformed monkey
with clairvoyant
                    prowess?

these porcupine
variations multi-
contrived the
          labyrinthine

hanged himself
                    in situ
doppelgänger-twin
sluiced within
concentric meatgrinder

I drew a match
shorter than the rest
                    after all

tacky mystery tour
with bogus spiritual
cicerone to boot

so enough of lurid
laughing gas, poetaster

couched in bunker no. 4
as if
between the cherubim

3

whirlwind of
fragmentary
dust irrepressible
    plague of locusts

the child reciting
the Seventh Seal
    laughs like a
    mischievous imp

apokalupsis apocatastasis
soteriology in its
unmaking completes
    the final circle

this *Zona* has wheels
within wheels flames
    within flames

not even you can
rearrange this thread
of treacherous of
    theatrical thread

it is warning you
with its Chernobyl fog

emissions so
statuary so stealthy
    you'll be
intoxicated
instantaneously

what devious
    trajectory?
what arcane
    Escher tower?

escalation to

the dungeon?
What souterrain
    complications?

Crawling rat-wise
grease-flanked
inimitable scuffle
white scum atop
    the cesspond
congealing as
        frogspawn

ablutions of the
juridical waterfalls
reaped judgment
heaped upon a
    thousand pates

opening of the
multitudinous books

tissue interleaf
    interposed
justification's parchment
wafer of peerless
      penitence

4

Stalker stretched
    akimbo assuming
death's mask
last seizure of his
      universe

Beethoven's Ninth
locomotive-trundle
glasses' shift-
      rattle

what necromancy?
what inhumane
tinnitus, surcharge
of imp-breath left
    us dumbfounded?

writer astrophysicist
    debate critique
with scathing
accuracy across
    formica boards

multifariously
enlist kingdoms
of the world
encircling the Zone
    final ultimatum

discharge of nuclear
fallout Zyklon B
        ammonia

a final scramble
exhumation of
    prophet porcupine

hanged himself
in situ delivered
sibling-twin through
concentric
    meatgrinder

traces of red mud
scorched embryos
penetration of
    various
    "heliospheres"

Stalker's shaven pate
    couched within
spouse's lap like

a mildewy potato
    retching up phlegm

their supernatural
    spawn performs
warped miracles
in a mould-ridden
kitchen
    for no-one

5

black dog inverted
metamorphosis

precipitation within
    this holy-of-holies

sacred lintel
where Stalker
intones homiletics
    to silence

negative theology
is better than no
    theology at all

patient penumbras
panted petitions
last gasp
    glossolalia

Emmaus re-configured
within the
    cyber age

Logos unstutterable
    unmentionable

triad of ingrown

hatred brotherhood
        homo-sapien

between the cherubim
every desire can
                materialize?

imagistic integers
        completion
within the
        bunker of hades

it is warning you
with its pillar–
        of-fire smog

do not tempt the
        transcendental
with your inept
        immanence
cheapjack charity

not even the
burnished temple
can ensure
        containment
        after all

Seventh Seal
Latter Rain
                lucent

shattering
dislocated altars
of our
        finding

6

dislocated altars
preside over
stagnant
    life-rivers

Jerusalem
ruptured seizure
of seizures
nations
    fulminate

denizens of
the party of the
Latter Rain
assemble on a
parched plain
for one final
    reckoning

Stalkers will
rise and fall
a messianic
    transpiring

marachals of the
lamb marshals
of the wolf lost
battalions of
the tigon move
in stately
    anabasis

regal banners
flutter amber-wise
    flame-astute

environmentally
unfriendly their
torches solarised

along arid stony
         creek-beds

take this cup
garden of the
final
        abandonment

Stalker's labials
sandpaper dry
sputter out one
last prophecy as
        curdled vomit

that no haruspex
will bother to
interpret in
charismatic
        spasm

whilst his sole
offspring deformed
Jeanne d'Arc
of the final
        dispensation

acerbic amputee
monkey queen
walking on the
                waters

redemptrix regis
returns to the
Room *la Zona*
as if to her
private enceiled
        boudoir

a meteor?
a kingdom
        coming?

slithers of
encrypted glass

in the dust
millennial
      stirrings
cyphers of

    ersatz
        morning

FOUR

Chapel of Rest
after Picasso's *The Death of Casagemas*

On that day in 2006 a room in Lund,
near Malmo, was the portal, the very
hinge of my earthly duration

With expressionist vigour
let the painted light splinter
        and spray.

One candle. Maybe two.

Your sepulchral profile, in this
vestibule, the only self-controlled,
        pacified set of features
                available.

Yet I would subjugate you to
        no enforced mummery.

There are no cyphers here just
the transcendental frustrations or
        unknowable raptures that lead
to yet more darkly-illuminated
                cirrus-clouds.

Yet this is no Book of Hours for an
early, millennial malaise. Just
        fragments of a liturgical
murmuring that has somehow
             escaped the burning.

In seeing your vacant corpus,
placated here, I begin to learn the
        art of living this penultimate
passage. Unconsciously.

For your Chapel of Rest was, indeed,
the very atrium-womb of our
        miscellaneous arrivals and
                departures.

A chrysalis where metamorphosis
        was marginally possible.

Personal Mountains
after Keith Jarrett / for Patrick Anderson

1

Those were Alps,
    Magus-processionals,
        caravanserai of the
utmost self-discoveries.

So: I bided my time.

Logos-proliferations
    doppelgänger-disjunctions.

So the light shone through
    periodically;

a luminous bar
    grazing our rough
        shoulders.

Descent becomes
    a Song of Ascents.

A descant
    counter-intuitively
working its power
        into the weave.

This rhythm; that rhythm.

Eastern periplum;
    wintering in a pagoda-

                              hostel.
Fasting, imbibing pills of
         the most polite
passiveness;
                          your chemically-
         balancing sabbatical.

So now I follow your
                  pioneering legs'
acclimatisation

                  on Primrose Hill.

2

Your airborne-rhythm;
               my earth-bound rhythm:

         our idiosyncratic icons?

Unsynchronised
         counterweave of
                     cross-purposes;
sheer delight of
         agon-antiphon.

An aesthetics of tension,
               steeled fortitude.

My Neoplatonism
         and/or
         your Social Darwinism.

What configurations?
         tangled figure-of-eights?

What Gordian,
               what Celtic knots
border this vacuum
               of negative space?

We circumambulate
    the various summits,
achieve altitudes of
    assumption,
        alterity,
            acclamation.

Your Moses bush?
    your pate for heights?

A vulture's view of Sinai
    (envenomed) can
    surely be deceptive;

the warped fuselage
    bucking its *gravitas*.

Take me back to the
    walled city, its hidden nest.

Where the escritoire,
    the ink-well
        compose

dynamic still lifes
    of

    sedentary seers.

3

Staccato jabs at the
        keyboard;
    haunched-up,
        predatory.

Confederate with the
        Rain Dogs.

Electrical curlicues'
    song of ascents;

scales of innovation
relapse into a
sonorous silence.

Regression the only
modal progression here.

Declension, intonation
and my inflections'
reflexiveness;

Chalk Farm on a late
Sunday
matutinal.

Afterwards
your metropolitan jaunts
trekking the
tortured tarmacadam

for what seemed an aeon
to find the choicest
vegetarian eatery.

My penchant for
exhibitions, an aesthete
only to be satiated by
metaphysical bread alone.

Counter-posed, the
major-minor fugue
in all its dual motion;

the in-built laws
of improvisation.

Poems rhythmically
syncopated even

from the beginning
of the Word.

4

So the fuselage bucked;
some goaded behemoth
　　　　trucking its refusals.

We slipped through the
　　　　hot railings, played
　　motley in a park
　　　　of earthly delights

until I slipped off the
　　　　mountains of reason.

Time is a delusive
　　　　juggernaut; these cogs
　　have a tendency
　　　　　　to slip.

My annealed summit
　　simmers,
　　　　　it burbles.

Inquisitions will have
　　　　to falter,
　　as will requisitions.

For the composer or poet's
　　silence undoes
　　　　the attempted
　　　　　　auto-da-fe

　　in every single
　　　　　instance.

5

Where were our Zipporahs then
　　when we were
　　astride our
　　　　reflexive mountains?

Within a dense, camera-
        popping crowd I was
utterly stillborn
                in the Sistine.

Yet there were two maidens
        tête-à-tête
                at the well-head.

Whilst you preferred,
        I recall, the
        Roman psycho-geography.

What gashed self-reproach?

What fine choreographed
        line between a
                mistress and a
                        muse?

So we fostered respective
        solitudes, garnered
                solipsist
                        consolations;

became inveterate survivors
        from the heady
                'Nineties'.

Eschewing codification we
        astutely balanced
                our imbalances,

intuitively nursed
        generational stigmatas;

becoming rugged exiles
        within our own
                especial
                        hinterlands.

Finally comfortable within
    our own suit of skins;

armoured for any
    belligerent

                          mountain.

Oasis

after Keith Jarrett / for Suzanne Norman

1

Escalier,
            at the turn of;
fabled, aleatory
                  rendezvous.

Your feints, teeth-glimmer;
my braggadocio
                  stumbling.

Gashed well-head:

masquerading, metaphysical
      Moses-maker;
all maimed and medieval,
            marked for suffering.

Gorgeous Zipporah,
      gorgeous insouciance;
queen of pragmatism,
      Eleatic empress of
            multi-haberdasheries;

those pre-conscious
            gambits flailing.

Commission Piero;
      a double portrait for
            wrecked posterity.

Primeval flautist's
    prelude; all mock-operatic.

A Brechtian burlesque,
    a time out of psychoses.

Ingress, egress
    out of that
        infernal machine.

Each other's
    necessary
        wellspring.

2

Each other's drypoint
    lineaments,
        sibylline-tracery;

your sheer elegance,
        exquisite stylistics.

My tongue: the ready penman,
        able ambassador.

What calligraphy of longing,

typography of servitude
        was there?

So you re-wrote the
    annals of curvature
        as the deer pants.

Similitude,
    lace-work of water,
    some fluid architecture;

these prehensile oracles
    of our apprehensive love.

A mumbled glossolalia
  attaining to crystal
   coherence

on the mute cylinders

   of screeching Amour.

3

Negative espousals;
   not necessarily.

Elongated, legendary
  journey through sheer
  glacier-ice
    or sand.

Maimed-solitary:
  the infant single, or
    the mourning twin?

I am the water-carrier,
  she said demurely.
In some codexes I am
  emblematic of streams
   and rivers.

Stroking her arched back
  I felt the liquid sinew;

the rest:
   a bodily redemption.

An appliqué of
    eros–cum–agape.

Watch the manuscript
    bleed.

After all, maybe I was alone
        treading these grapes
                of fulmination?

Maybe you were the
        mirage of miracle?

Phanopoeia is not overly
        concerned with cadence.

And *melopoeia* is, altogether,
        an abstract enterprise.

Only takes milli-seconds
        for your *san graal*

                to be drained.

4

After the imbibing
        sluggish inability
                to travel on.

Time's honed fuselage
        commandeering all
                available space.

Dynamic-static:
        a lame, mutual
                dependence is all.

This sheath has ensured
        no superior 'shining'
                can occur?

Your technology most steely,
                dear.

Who could foresee a

serious dethroning?

Anyway,
      usurpation might prove
      post-traumatical.

And the Angel of History
      waves its toy-pistol like
some crazed partisan
      as we all dutifully
                        applaud.

Lepers and madmen
      had the truth pouched
in their bindles
                  after all.

Hysteria mounts Reason
      as the infernal machine:
      clinical, codified, clicks

on to its latest

                  commodity

      punctual as mean-time.

You grin your supreme grin,
      resplendent Aquitaine.

Let my lips ideogram
            your cool cheek;

allow me to top the bill
      again in your

                  Courts of Love.

5

Cellular intercourse and
  transmitted encomiums;

the luminous salutations
    sputtering.

Wavelengths compatible-
   incompatible.

You playing
  Eleanor the Untouchable.
And me: some radio messiah-
     poet.

All a succinct charade, a
  virtually divested rehearsal
for this genuinely fleshed-out
    oasis trysting.

Sucking out the quintessence,
  the *energeia*.

What pith? what marrow?

And should I pigeon-hole this
  for perverse sister,
    Posterity?

Or should I merely decline,
a spent David beneath
  the myrtles of bathos?

Or take this fibreglass harp,
  recycle it into some
  installation of
    the injured Id?

There are regenerate galleries
  in the most unsuspected
    cosmic regions.

Psycho-geographical burrs
    emanating from Bosch's
        Concert in the Ovum;

travelling from, and to, an
    utterly inconceivable

           Godhead.

6

Date-cakes, honeyed offerings,
    your venous unction;

going halves on a Chardonnay-
        Shiraz.

Calypso or Circe? So you
    preside regardless within
        an impeccable grotto.

Shrouded in your claustral
    hood, your numinous glow.

And me: an Homeric 'No-Man', a
    detainee, with nowhere else
        left to linger or go.

Communing within the cool
warmth of your
        practical nimbus;

vouchsafing to
        'go under'.

Balm oils, multi-channels,
    pharmaceuticals;

honoured by a 'palm-leaf'
    nonchalance, understated
tabernacle of
        quiet eroticism;

whilst your ess-shaped, exquisite,
    fawn-like 'posture'
implants its plethora of

      urban legends.

7

Having traversed Lethe;

cardinal virtues choreograph
    their parabolic triads.

Rose petals pepper
      this indigo surface...

Whilst I encounter
    feminine fulmination,
      red-hot throne-chariots;

    your barbed hemispheres.

So I brood with the worst of them;

misanthropically nursing
    my sore art in this
    self-excluded
      abnegation.

Paradiso terrestre:
    misnomer for an infernal,
self-fulfilling prophecy
      then?

Take me back
    via the Wood of Suicides
before, beyond
    mind's catastrophic
      deforestation.

Whose overthrow

(yours, mine)?
whose love anyway?

Forgetting the truly benign
     universals as well as the
          malignant particulars

takes more than
          vital breath
                    away.

8

My hybrid, buoyant piano;
     your fluid soprano sax:

declensions,
     semi-quaverings,
     permutations
               like tesserae.

Sultry April night in Tokyo,
          late Seventies;

that incumbent era of our
     respective inceptions.

Middle England: her
               parched lowlands
     of provincial murmurs,
               fiscal discontents.

These modest steeples,
     ugly silos do not
portend an oasis or
               paradiso, do they?

Whilst we glide no closer
     to our desirous renewals;

as the shimmering *nous*

suggests an alternative,
        cyclical
                embarking.

Our configurations possess
        wrought stellar
                incantations.

You must perceive that, dear?

Fountains of inborn crystal,
        luminous Yggdrasills

blooming in flagrant disregard
        of their charred,
                trashy surroundings.

Meanwhile,
        our snatched communions

are surely somewhere
            to fortify,
        amass a prevalence of

            Amour.

9

Escalier,
        at the turn of;
fabled, *pre*determined

            rendezvous.

Coda

Chosen, Neoplatonic barque
       shearing wave-crest;

your cerebral pursuits
      always sensuously emanate.

This universe alive
     and trembling
          in the tireless
            wake.

You are light within that shade
    or, the patiently implied
        chiaroscuro.

For all things that are,
          are *lumina*; with

their restless, their
      curious

         unknowings.

FIVE

Lamentate

after Arvo Pärt's *Lamentate* & Anish Kapoor's *Marsyas*

(Minacciando)

All pretensions laid bare
like the unfurled
        crimson flesh.

A sepulchral mirrour,
        an arterial banner;
ruby corpuscle of
        torturous demise.

Arvo faces his own death
        in the Hall of Turbines.

A nakedness deeper than
        the nude's nudity.

Flayed like a deluxe satin purse
turned inside out
    vomit-spilling
        the innards crystalline.

Neoplatonic Apollo
    incensed somewhat?

Death the scarlet fuselage.

Raw carnage of our existence
eked out on the spiked looms.

Self-slaughter of

artist-persona
un-selfs self.

Sure, your doppelgänger's
always your harshest critic;

and yet I am not done

with living
yet.

(Spietate)

Not done with living or
rapid dying yet.

I cauterise bad art, slovenly
living as if it were a
sneaking bacilli;

shred incompetency's
mislaid arrogance;

worm-like polluting the
temple's lintel-stone.

Arvo sees himself as agonised,
as flayed Marsyas. Yet he is,
by far, more Apollonian

than this modest misgiving
would allow?

Through the twelve zones of
our distinct sensibility
have we come.

Jealousy, possessiveness:
arch-twins of Gehenna.

Rivalrous for aesthetic perfection

beyond dictates of
      evil and good.

Yet can *le mot juste* still function
      when governing flesh?

Apollonian Helios burns with
a Sophoclean ferocity; the

purged remnant is far
      more than
            dross.

(Fragile)

"Not the priest
      but the victim"

Perforated Adonis-Christ
      swaying on that pierced,
         piercing reed.

Messianic pretenders
      need not apply;

vulnerability is the auto-key
      in this unrehearsed
         pantomime.

And the flesh is as the livid sky
      in this

Hall of Turbines.

Cramoisi is so easily torn;

human frailty can be an
      overwhelming aesthetic-
      cum-spiritual strength
         it seems.

I lament the living worm
     not the corpse of the
          rotting lion.

There is no unwieldy fulcrum;

just this most spindly of
     millennium bridges to
give us anchorage
         here.

Flesh's earthy cornucopia
     is both horizontal
         and vertical;

its paradigm dependent on
     how taut it is pulled.

Feebleness our architectonics
     then.

Samson, in the barber's chair,
     is as composed as a

straitjacketed deserter.

Need you ask again
     why Arvo must lament

not the dead but
     the living
         organisms?

(Pregando)

Pleading for his wretched,
     arrogant life:

     Marsyas the Corpuscular.

Muses are offended,

Neoplatonic Apollo
maligned.

What judgement awaits
such a paltry poetaster?

An iambic-stunted
rhymester at best;

inflicting his crude doggerel
on the beautiful
and the refined.

To kalon degraded on the mart;

her brasserie of re-invention
soiled in his oozing pus.

Begging for forgiveness,
this pretentious jerk;

flailing now for
articulation's touch and the
mot juste that still

manages to elude his
phlegm-smeared labials.

Now a huge, flayed carcass
hovers above
like a neon sign

with no need under heaven
to plead for

your just

approvals.

(Solitudine – stato d'animo)

Only alone
        must you face death.

Only alone must you
    endure
        your living.

Nous: the universe's
        vital component, declares
this within the
        very firmament.

Arvo, perceiving this in
        the Hall of Turbines,

composed mid-mind
    desires for life and a

        Lament for the Living.

Universe enthroned,
        cosmos enlivened;

intelligence burbling
    in the vegetable world.

Courage to, once more,
    pick up
        the lyre.

(Consolante)

After the excoriations,
    that grey-eyed nymph,
angelus novus so
        pleasing to the eye,

attended me;
    ravens brought me

morsels of wholemeal.

So I revived under her
             medicinal digits.

In the level place of
             luscious verbenas
I re-emerged within
             the universal *nous*.

Through the twelve zones
             of our distinct sensibility
                         have we come...

And the domes were riveted
             with yarns of gold...

And the argent slates flashed
             in light so granular.

Haemorrhaging ceased, my
             chapped nakedness
concealed beneath a clean
             raiment, the
                         whitest of whites...

And I turned to her and said:
             is this the
                         paradiso terrestre?

And she, sweet paradigm
             of purest water:

speak not of the unknown, the
             transcendental, for to do so
will only deaden your sense
             of wondrous
                         perception.

Merely record
             apperception's

as if capturing the effects
of light within a
                    modulating crystal.

For you yourself are the
            wrought cypher in full
                    state of both

            refraction and reception.

Yet your purging must, for
            a further season, begin
                        once more.

For now you are as one
            capsuled within the
                    very
                        filaments...

(Stridendo)

Agonistic choreography;
            contrapuntal clash
                    of artistries.

Lute necks that gleam
                    prodigious.

So Marsyas and Apollo
            size up each other's
reedy instruments
                with a mutual envy.

Diatribes, flytings;
what resounding
                symphonic stridency
                    echoes here?

Metaphysical invades the

physical; refined Neoplatonic

imbues the clammy,
    tentacular clays of
        Adamic earth.

Marsyas' song positively seethes:
    a crude rendition worthy

of a drunk carousing a whore,
    is still an unlikely
        Carmina Burana.

Apollo, meanwhile, soars
    in Dantescan aethers as if

emanating acoustically
    the spheres of the sun.

Of course,
    the plaited laurels will
impress his crisp,
        wavy curlicues.

And nothing can come from
counterpoint but art's
    just and punitive
        retributions.

In short: passive Marsyas's
    slow, but deliberate,
skinning, in these

    active, solarised rays
    of
        no mercy.

(Lamentabile)

Alone you will hang
    in the vacuum
       taut as a scarlet parachute.

Alone you will dangle:
    a silky stillborn afterbirth.

Stripped raw-hide,
    one huge scab of
       divine fulmination.

Bi-polarised;
    wrenched between pride
    and self-loathing.

Estranged,
your creations amass:
    an anabasis of nations all

       ready to take you on.

Without warning
your discreetly gilded chariot
    transforms into an
       egocentric gibbet

all ready to tighten; but
    love's martyrdom
       somehow eludes you with

a terminal precision,
    as you experience
divine usurpation
       ad infinitum.

Unwillingly
    you are caressed by
ten thousand
       noli me tangeres.

Forced to fast-track a
million
via dolorosas

in the vestibule of the
elongated skull.

Artfully slung
between two thieves and
panting out your
pathetic fallacies;

the messianic hour of *tenebrae*
is nothing compared to
your orgasm of
latter rain.

A brimstone precipitation
pounds its
awkward theodicy in the

phylactery of your
inner ear-drum.

Soon you will be
dispensationally arranging
time
like a calculating
Angel of the Millennium.

The millstone slides around
your sleek neck
as you tread

the mesmerising
waters of
Phlegethon.

An unauthorised refugee
in your own familial
homestead;

a chronic contemplative
chewing on the
      embittered black bread

of your sublime
            orphanhood.

(Risolutamente)

So who will re-thread the
      trembling arteries?
Re-position the pulsing,
            frantic organs?

What will your exposed body,
your composer-hands,
      look like after the
            necessary purging?

And what will your scaled
      artistry amount to
when the eternal recurrence
            has occurred?

            Creator-source

      reabsorbs your
            luminous grimaces.

A redetermination to
      pick up the tired nib with
a spiritually-renewed
            energy.

This lament is for *all*
            the living.

Make sure that apophthegm is
      preserved inscription.

Just as the piano leaps

triadic beyond the
                    orchestra;

as the individual soul is in
sheer state-of-becoming
        one with the universal *nous*.

Your innate failures are
        actually
                arcane apertures
                of a realised success.

This flayed carcass is indeed
        the primed cocoon of
                    la vita nuova;

but you are still
        unconscious of certain
                phenomena.

As Apollo and Marsyas
        re-unite as two halves
        of the
                    Parnassian stratosphere:

the Corporeal and the
        Immaterial organum.

Contrapuntal resolution
        is everything this collective
                body can hear...

each nuanced to their own
        contemplative mode...

the trefoiled layers of
        the
                Mystical Rose.

(Fragile e concilante)

Into the silence after the
    reeds' salutary music.

What is left to us?

Incandescent nymphs have
    retired to their
        hermetic groves;

    are hushed for a while.

Whilst we are re-animated
    with *Contemplatio*.

Exactly; this universe is
alive with an intelligence
    which is often
        beyond us.

Our faculties' indigence,
    the *nous*' impassivity

pervades our radiant cosmos
    with its innately
        divine fire.

Suffering is holiness.

That much is certain.

Laments are cast for our
    ultimate felicity;

    we who live, that is.

The craftsmen work with
    an internal joy
        burbling.

For the signature of the
    divine calligraphically

imbues all
　　　heliocentric creation.

Not done with living
　　　or rapid dying yet.

As the divine fire quickens
　　us in the latter hour

　　of our study-sessions.

Most excellent genera;
　　arcana not confined to
　　　　the adytum.

All pretensions laid bare
　　and superbly
　　　　incinerated.

The divinity hovers above
　　　　the lotus;

　　take that for kerygma.

To become one,
　　　quite perfected,

with the Rose of
　　pure, most mellifluous

　　　　flame.

Notes

1

In Principio – *In Principio* is a 2003 composition by Arvo Pärt (b. 1935) for chorus and orchestra setting a Latin text from the Gospel of John (1:1-14).

'periplum': a word used and partially coined by the poet Ezra Pound (1885-1972) in his epic poem *The Cantos* to refer to a 'voyage' or 'journey'. The original Greek prefix simply means 'around' or 'about'.

'Castor, Pollux': in Greek mythology Castor and Pollux were the twin sons of Leda.

'Philemon and Baucis': an old married couple in Ovid's *Metamorphoses* who were the only people in their town to welcome the disguised gods Jupiter and Mercury. As a reward their cottage was turned into a temple or a chapel. The couple were eventually metamorphosed into an oak and a linden.

'san graal': French for 'holy grail'.

'chiliastically': an adverb coined by the author with a play on the noun 'chiliast' meaning 'millenarian' or 'a thousand years'.

'*The Enneads*': the collected works of Neoplatonic philosopher Plotinus (c.204–270).

'Demiurgus': Latin for 'demiurge'; a concept from the Platonic, Neopythagorean and Neoplatonic schools of philosophy for an artisan-like figure responsible for the creation and maintenance of the physical universe.

'Nous': equated to the intellect or intelligence in philosophical thinking and associated with intuition and perception.

'le mot juste': French for 'the right word'.

'terrae': plural of 'terra' i.e. Earth, third planet from the Sun.

'Nekuia': in ancient Greek cult-practice and literature a "rite by which ghosts were called up and questioned about the future," Homer's *Odyssey* XI is perhaps the most famous example of a *nekuia*.
'Apollonius': Apollonius of Tyana (c.15- c.100) was a Greek Neopythagorean philosopher.

The Lord's Supper – deliberately written in a style similar to the ancestral and ethno- poems collected in Jerome Rothenberg's *Poland/1931* (1974).

The Elders – deliberately written in a style similar to Geoffrey Hill's poem *The Apostles* (from the sequence *Of Commerce and Society*) to be found in his debut collection *For the Unfallen* (1959).

2

The Angel of History – the epigraph by Walter Benjamin is taken from his collection of essays *Illuminations*.
'Dada': an art movement of the European avant-garde in the early 20th Century. Originating in 1915 as a reaction to the horrors of World War One. It prized nonsense, irrationality and intuition over reason and logic in order to subvert hegemonies of power.
'Vorticism': a Modernist British art and literary movement which occurred in London during World War One and which was led by Wyndham Lewis, Ezra Pound and Henri Gaudier-Brzeska. International in flavour and inspired by Cubism it was arguably the most dynamic British art movement of the 20th Century.
'The Golden Calf': *The Cave of the Golden Calf* was an avant-garde cabaret and night club in London just off Regent Street which was opened in 1912 and quickly became a haunt for aristocrats, artists and bohemians. The Club was low-ceilinged and appropriately sunk beneath pavement level. Jacob Epstein, Wyndham Lewis, Ezra Pound and Eric Gill were all, at one time, members. Gill designed and sculpted a calf which would become the club's trademark motif and is still exhibited in galleries today. Due to bankruptcy *The Cave* closed in 1914 but became the solid model for future night clubs. Its uncanny similarity to a certain subterranean 'Brit Pop' club of the mid-nineties also located on Regent Street can not be overlooked.

'Timon': an allusion to Wyndham Lewis' Cubo-Futurist illustrations for Shakespeare's *Timon of Athens* (1912).

'John Amos Darby': *alter ego* of the author.

'Aquitaine' – Eleanor of Aquitaine (1124-1204) was Duchess of Aquitaine and later Queen Consort of both England and France.

'Ventadorn' - Bernart de Ventadorn (1130-90) was a prominent troubadour who wrote love chansons for Eleanor.

'Mina Loy': Mina Löwry (1882–1966) was a Futurist poet, artist and bohemian. She was the last of the early Modernists to be posthumously recognised although Ezra Pound admired her work during her lifetime.

'H.D.': Hilda Doolittle (1886-1961) was an American poet and novelist who was associated with Ezra Pound's avant-garde Imagist movement in London during the early part of the 20th century.

'*Maestà*': a Sienese commisioned altarpiece composed of many individual paintings by Duccio di Buoninsegna (c.1255-1319). Three of these paintings can be viewed in the Sainsbury Wing of the National Gallery, London.

'*l'avventura*': Italian for 'the adventure'.

'Lucian Freud's model dances': Freud's famous model, the performance artist Leigh Bowery (1961-94) would often be seen in London clubs during the early nineties dancing with a wooden block strapped to one foot.

'Janey Morris, Lizzie Siddal'; models, muses and wives of Pre-Raphaelite artists William Morris and Dante Gabriel Rossetti.

'Kafkan': adjective coined by the author to suggest something resembling a character or situation from one of Franz Kafka's novels or short stories.

'Hourglass sanatoriums': phrase borrowed from the title of a 1973 film by Polish director Wojciech Has.

'Raskolnikov': the anti-hero protagonist of Fyodor Dostoyesky's *Crime and Punishment* (1866).

'Latter Rain': a term used in Holiness and Pentecostal movements especially during the 1880s.

3.

Earth – *Earth* is a 1930 Soviet film by Ukrainian director Aleksander Dovzhenko about the process of Bolshevik collectivization.

The Library Hovers Above Solaris – *Solaris* is a 1972 science fiction art film by Russian director Andrei Tarkovsky based on the novel of the same name by Stanislaw Lem. Much of the imagery and ideas of *The Library Hovers Above Solaris* are inspired by, and based on, the visual and sonic emanations of the film. There are also additional musings on aspects of scientific exploration of the cosmos during the latter half of the 20th Century and beyond. Tarkovsky's film concentrates upon the thoughts and the consciences of cosmonaut scientists studying the planet Solaris' mysterious ocean which is able to materialise simulacra of people the cosmonauts know or have known. The library aboard their space-station is used by Tarkovsky as the microcosm of all of human and earthly civilisation.

'Kung': another name for Chinese sage and philosopher Confucius.

'*Übermenschen*': German for 'Overman' a concept in the philosophy of Friedrich Nietzsche.

'Antiochus has polluted the temple': an allusion to the so-called 'abomination of desolation' recorded in Jewish rabbinical literature when Antiochus IV Epiphanes erected a statue to Zeus in the sacred precincts of the Second Temple in Jerusalem.

'cabined, cribbed': an allusion to a line in Shakespeare's *Macbeth* (Act 3, Scene 4).

'Rublev's *Apokalypse*': an allusion to Tarkovsky's 1966 film *Andrei Rublev*.

'*Shekinah*': denotes the 'dwelling' or 'settling' of the divine presence of God. 'Shekinah' is the English spelling of a grammatically feminine Hebrew ancient blessing.

The Zone – *Stalker* is a 1979 science fiction art film by Russian director Andrei Tarkovsky based on the novel *Roadside Picnic* by Boris and Arkady Strugatsky. As with the previous poem the imagery and ideas of *The Zone* are inspired by Tarkovsky's film in which the 'Stalker' is a professional guide to the Zone, someone who crosses the border into the forbidden Zone with a specific goal and usually accompanied by paying and curious 'pilgrims' (in the film *Stalker* these are 'Writer' and 'Scientist').

'*apokalupsis*': Greek for 'apocalypse'; an 'uncovering' or 'revealing'.

'*apocatastasis*': Greek for 'restitution' or 'reconstitution'. Used by Neoplatonists and Christian Universalists to describe 'a restoration to the original or primordial condition'.

'Chernobyl fog': an allusion to the catastrophic nuclear accident that happened on 26th April 1986 at the Chernobyl Nuclear Power Plant in the Ukraine. The similarity to the situation presented in Tarkovsky's *Stalker* can not be overlooked.

'Seventh Seal': Revelation 8:1. Also an allusion to Ingmar Bergman's 1955 film of the same name.

4

Chapel of Rest - Picasso's *The Death of Casagemas* was completed in 1901 after Picasso's close friend had committed suicide and depicts Casagemas' profile as he lays on his death-bed. His friend's untimely death had a seismic impact on Picasso and there are several paintings from the *Blue* and *Rose* periods that explore the subsequent pain and guilt he experienced.

Personal Mountains – *Personal Mountains* is a 1979 composition by Keith Jarrett which was released on two live albums. This musical piece provided the initial rhythms, title and starting point for this 'personal' poem of friendship.

' Rain Dogs': *Rain Dogs* is a 1985 song and album title by Tom Waits.

'Zipporahs': Zipporah was Moses' Midianite wife who opposed the circumcision of their son (Exodus 2:21 / 4:25-26).

'Yet there were two maidens / tête-à-tête / at the well-head': *Scenes from the Life of Moses*, Sandro Botticelli, c. 1481/82. Rome, Sistine Chapel.

Oasis – *Oasis* is a 1979 composition by Keith Jarrett which was released on three live albums. This musical piece provided the initial rhythms, title and starting point for this 'personal' poem of love and friendship.

'*Escalier*': French for 'staircase'.

'Piero': Piero della Francesca (1415-92) was an Italian painter of the Early Renaissance.

'*Phanopoeia*': a literary term coined by Ezra Pound to define the "casting of images upon the visual imagination" within poetry.

'*melopoeia*': a literary term coined by Ezra Pound to define when "words are charged, over and above their plain meaning, with some musical property" within poetry.

'Aquitaine': Eleanor of Aquitaine (1124-1204); see note above.

'Bosch's / Concert in the Ovum': *Concert in the Egg* is a 1561 copy of a painting by Hieronymous Bosch.

'Homeric 'No-Man'': Odysseus in Homer's *Odyssey*.

'Sultry April night in Tokyo, / late Seventies': an allusion to the Keith Jarrett performance captured on his live album *Sleeper* which was the starting point for the poem.

'Yggdrasills': Yggdrasill is the name of an immense mythical tree which was central in Norse cosmology.

Coda - 'For all things that are, / are *lumina*': paraphrase of a quotation from philosopher Scotus Eriugena's (c. 815-77) *Periphyseon (The Division of Nature)* which is also quoted and referenced in Ezra Pound's *Cantos*.

'*lumina*': Latin for 'light'.

5

Lamentate – *Lamentate* is a 2002 composition by Arvo Pärt for piano and orchestra which was inspired by Anish Kapoor's colossal art-installation *Marsyas*. Arvo Pärt wrote in the liner notes for *Lamentate*: "When I first saw *Marsyas* by Anish Kapoor at the opening of the exhibition, October 2002, in the Turbine Hall of Tate Modern in London, the impact that it had upon me was a powerful one. My first impression was that I, as a living being, was standing before my own body and was dead – as in a time-warp perspective, at once in the future and the present. Suddenly, I found myself put into a position in which my life appeared in a different light. In this moment I had a strong sense of not being ready to die. And I was moved to ask myself just what I could still manage to accomplish in the time left to me.

Death and suffering are the themes that concern every person born into this world. The way in which the individual comes to terms with these issues (or fails to do so) determines his attitude towards life – whether – consciously or unconsciously.

With its great size, Anish Kapoor's sculpture shatters not only concepts of space, but also – in my view – concepts of time. The boundary between time and timelessness no longer seems so evident. This is the subject matter underlying my composition

Lamentate. Accordingly, I have written a lamento – not for the dead, but for the living, who have to deal with these issues for themselves. A lamento for us, struggling with the pain and hopelessness of this world."

The poem *Lamentate* is a response and 'homage' to both Arvo Pärt's *Lamentate* and Anish Kapoor's *Marsyas* whilst also being an attempt to forge a semantic 'Lament for the Living'.

'Marsyas': in Greek mythology Marsyas challenged the god Apollo to a contest of music and for his audacity was killed by being flayed alive.

'mirrour': the original English spelling for 'mirror' derived from Middle English and French.

'"Not the priest / but the victim"': a quotation from Allen Upward cited and embedded by Pound in to *The Cantos*.

'*To kalon*': Greek for 'the beautiful'.

'*Carmina Burana*': a manuscript of 254 poems and dramatic texts from the 11th and 12th Centuries which are mostly bawdy, irreverent and satirical.

'*tenebrae*' – Latin for 'darkness' or 'shadows'.

'dispensationally': an adverb coined by the author with a play on the noun 'despensation' used in Christian theology and meaning 'a divinely ordained order prevailing at a particular period of history'.

Acknowledgements

Thanks to: James Goddard, Seb Doubinsky, Paul Stubbs, Blandine Longre, Andrew O'Donnell, Will Stone, Michael Lee Rattigan, Sarah Roberts, Patrick Anderson, Suzanne Norman, Jenny Warner, Katie Timoshenko, Rob Graves, Andrew & Hannah Pattison and my parents.

Thanks to Ann Graves for proofreading this manuscript.

This book is dedicated to Suzanne
whether she comprehends it or not

"Each other's
necessary
wellspring"

About the Author

Mark Wilson has previously published two poetry collections: *Quartet For the End of Time* (*Editions du Zaporogue,* 2011) and *Passio* (*Editions du Zaporogue,* 2013). Both are available to buy or download at www.lulu.com. Mark studied English Literature at Goldsmiths, University of London, during the 1990s where his dissertation was on language-renewal within the poetry of Ezra Pound. His poems and articles have appeared in *The Black Herald, The Shop, 3:AM Magazine, The Fiend* and *Le Zaporogue*.

More Poetry & Lyrics From
Leaky Boot Press

Mothballs: Quantum Poems
Seb Doubinsky

Mothballs: Quantum Poems is the long awaited new collection by the internationally acclaimed poet Seb Doubinsky.

"The whole collection. . . reads as one long poem with pauses in between (the white noise of daily life) and then these snapshots of sheer magic that radiate with a synaesthesia of all the senses intermingling- words, breath, the ticking of the clock. There is such a pulse in these lines. . ."

Cynthia Atkins, author of
Psyche's Weathers and *In the Event of Full Disclosure*

ISBN: 978-1-909849-00-6

The Kindest Lies: the Lyrics of John Lyle
John Lyle

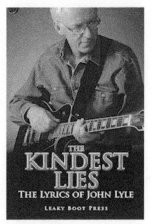

Reading like the best kind of poetry—moving, emotive, wistful, relevant and often funny—the lyrics of Canadian singer-songwriter John Lyle throw our world and our lives into sharp focus.

Not but a shadow
Hold my world of stormy care

There is never time to waste in this holy place, which is this land we live in. This life, this vast landscape of the heart. Those are John's words and Woody would concur and so would all of the great poets. The valley might be lonesome and the blossoms might be broken but to John Lyle they will always scent the morning air. Always. And to me, this lies at the heart of John's art.

Matt Bialer, author of *Bridge*

ISBN: 978-1-909849-01-3